EASY ITALIAN PHRASE BOOK

770 Basic Phrases for Everyday Use

DOVER PUBLICATIONS, INC.
NEW YORK

Copyright

Published in Canada by General Publishing Company, Ltd., 30 Lesmill Road, Don Mills, Toronto, Ontario.
Published in the United Kingdom by Constable and Company, Ltd., 3 The Lanchesters, 162–164 Fulham Palace Road, London W6 9ER.

Bibliographical Note

The material in this book was originally published by Dover in 1957 as part of a manual to accompany a recording entitled *Listen & Learn Italian*. The English outline was prepared by the editorial staff of Dover Publications, Inc. The Italian translation and transliteration were prepared by Olga Ragusa.

Library of Congress Cataloging-in-Publication Data

Easy Italian phrase book : 770 basic phrases for everyday use.
p. cm.
"Originally published by Dover in 1957 as part of a manual to accompany a recording entitled Listen & learn Italian. The English outline was prepared by the editorial staff of Dover Publications, Inc. The Italian translation and transliteration were prepared by Olga Ragusa"—T.p. verso.
Includes index.
ISBN 0-486-28085-3
1. Italian language—Conversation and phrase books—English. I. Dover Publications, Inc.
PC1121.E24 1994
458.3'421—dc20 94–15609
CIP

Manufactured in the United States of America
Dover Publications, Inc., 31 East 2nd Street, Mineola, N.Y. 11501

CONTENTS

INTRODUCTION

This book is designed to teach you the basic words, phrases and sentences that you will need for simple everyday communication in Italy. It does not attempt to teach you the grammatical structure of Italian, but instead helps you to express your needs and handle problems encountered while traveling.

The value of the book rests as much on what is omitted as on what is included. An effort has been made to include only those phrases pertinent to the needs of the traveler. You will find the phrase "May I have some small change" (a frequent need in travel), but do not expect to find a sentence like "This is the pen of my aunt." Furthermore, since the material presented here is not cumulative, as it is in conventional foreign-language courses, you need not start at the beginning. Study whichever phrases will be the most useful to you.

The focus of instruction is on what *you* will say. However, the section entitled "Making Yourself Understood," which contains such vital phrases as "Please speak more slowly" and "Repeat it, please," will aid you in understanding others.

This book is complete in itself and is meant to be used for reference and study. Read it at odd moments and try to learn ten or fifteen phrases a day. Also, be sure to take the manual with you when you go abroad. All that you have learned will be available for reference and review.

The book is designed to help you form additional Italian sentences from the sentences it provides. You can do this by substituting a new word for a given word in a familiar sentence. In sentences where this is possible, the candidate for substitution appears in brackets, and is sometimes followed by possible alternatives. For example,

I am [a student]
—a teacher
—a businessman

provides three sentences: "I am a student," "I am a teacher" and "I am a businessman."

Another especially helpful feature is the extensive topic and word index beginning on page 65. Notice that each entry in the book is numbered and that the index refers to these numbers. This enables you to locate information you need quickly, without having to search the entire page.

ITALIAN PRONUNCIATION

This book uses a phonetic transcription as an aid to correct pronunciation. (See "Scheme of Pronunciation," below.) It usually appears below the Italian line in the text.

Double Consonants

In Italian, a double consonant is longer in duration than its single counterpart. It is important to observe this distinction, because the difference between a single and a double consonant can change the meaning of a word. For example, *nono* means "ninth," while *nonno* means "grandfather."

SCHEME OF PRONUNCIATION

Letters	Transcription	Example	Notes
a	ah	as in f*a*ther	
b	b	as in *b*at	
c	k	as in s*k*in	*c* is pronounced *k* before *a, o, u* or *h*. Do not make a puff of air after the *k* as we do in English.
	ch	as in *ch*ur*ch*	*c* is pronounced *ch* before *i* or *e*.

Letters	Transcription	Example	Notes
d	d	as in *d*ental	Formed by touching the tongue tip to the teeth, not to the gum ridge behind the teeth as we do in English.
e	e OR eh (open)	as in m*e*t	
	ay (closed)	as in g*a*te, but cut short	Pronounce *ay* as a single pure sound, not a diphthong; do not slide over into an *ee* sound as we do in English.
f	f	as in *f*ate	
g	g	as in *g*o	*g* is pronounced *g* before *a, o, u* or *h*.
	j	as in *j*oke	*g* is pronounced *j* before *i* or *e*.
gl	ly	as in te*ll y*ou	Pronounce *ly* as a single sound.
gn	ny	as in ca*ny*on	Pronounce *ny* as a single sound.
h	—	—	*h* is always silent in Italian.
i	ee	as in f*ee*d, but cut short	Pronounce *ee* as a single pure sound, not a diphthong; do not slide over into a *y* sound as we do in English.
l	l	as in *l*et	never like the "dark" *l* in coo*l*.
m	m	as in *m*et	
n	n	as in *n*et	
o	aw (open)	as in l*aw*yer, but cut short	
	o OR oh (closed)	as in n*o*tify, but cut short	Pronounce *o* or *oh* as a single pure vowel, not a diphthong; do not slide over into an *oo* sound as we do in English.
p	p	as in s*p*in	Do not make a puff of air after the *p* as we do in English.

Letters	Transcription	Example	Notes
qu	kw	as in *qu*ick	
r	r	somewhat like in *r*ed	The Italian *r* is trilled with the tip of the tongue.
s	s	as in *s*ay	
	z	as in zeal	*s* is pronounced z before *b, d, g, l, m, n, r, v* and between vowels.
sc	sh	as in *sh*op	*sc* is pronounced *sh* before *i* or *e*.
	sk	as in *sk*irt	*sc* is pronounced *sk* elsewhere.
t	t	as in s*t*op	Formed by touching the tongue tip to the teeth, not to the gum ridge behind the teeth as we do in English. Do not make a puff of air after the *t*.
u	oo	as in f*oo*d, but cut short	Pronounce *oo* as a single pure vowel, not a diphthong; do not slide over into a *w* sound as we do in English.
v	v	as in *v*est	
x	ks	as in la*cks*	
z	ts	as in ca*ts*	The rules for when to pronounce *z* as *ts* and when to pronounce it as *dz* are complex. Follow the transcription to ensure correct pronunciation.
	dz	as in a*dz*e	

NOTE: The *u* and *i* of Italian diphthongs *uo* and *ie* are represented by *w* and *y* respectively. For example: Buono (*BWAW-no*), lieto (*LYEH-toh*).

Diphthongs written as REH‿ee, LEH‿ee, ah‿oo are to be pronounced as one syllable with no break between the two vowel sounds.

SOCIAL CONVERSATION

1. Good morning.
Buon giorno.
bwawn JOHR-no.

2. Good evening.
Buona sera.
BWAW-nah SAY-rah.

3. Good night.
Buona notte.
BWAW-nah NAWT-tay.

4. Hello.
Ciao.
CHYAH‿O.

5. Goodbye.
Addio.
ahd-DEE-o.

6. I'll be seeing you.
Arrivederci.
ahr-ree-vay-DAYR-chee.

7. I'll see you later.
A più tardi.
ah pyoo TAHR-dee.

8. So long.
Ciao.
CHYAH‿O.

9. I wish to make an appointment with Mr. Silvi.
Vorrei fare un appuntamento col signor Silvi.
vohr-REH‿ee FAH-ray oon ahp-poon-tah-MAYN-toh kohl see-NYOHR SEEL-vee.

10. May I introduce [Mr.] Mrs., Miss Silvi?
Posso presentarle [il signor] la signora, la signorina Silvi?
PAWS-so pray-zayn-TAHR-lay [eel see-NYOHR] lah see-NYOH-rah, lah se nyoh-REE-nah SEEL-vee?

11. —— my wife.
mia moglie.
MEE-ah MO-lyay.

12. —— my husband.
mio marito.
MEE-o mah-REE-toh.

13. —— my mother.
mia madre.
MEE-ah MAH-dray.

14. —— my father.
mio padre.
MEE-o PAH-dray.

15. —— my daughter.
mia figlia.
MEE-ah FEE-lyah.

16. —— my son.
mio figlio.
MEE-o FEE-lyoh.

17. —— my friend.
il mio amico (*masc.*).
eel MEE-o ah-MEE-ko.

18. —— my sister.
mia sorella.
MEE-ah so-REL-lah.

19. —— my brother.
mio fratello.
MEE-o frah-TEL-lo.

20. —— my children.
i miei bambini.
ee mee-EH‿ee bahm-BEE-nee.

21. I am glad to meet you.
Piacere di fare la sua conoscenza.
pyah-CHAY-ray dee FAH-ray lah SOO-ah ko-no-SHEN-tsah.

22. How are you?
Come sta?
KO-may stah?

23. Very well, thanks. And you?
Molto bene, grazie. E Lei?
MOHL-toh BEH-nay, GRAH-tsyay. ay LEH‿ee?

24. How are things?
Come va?
KO-may vah?

25. All right.
Bene.
BEH-nay.

26. So, so.
Così, così.
ko-ZEE, ko-ZEE.

27. How is your family?
Come sta la sua famiglia?
KO-may stah lah SOO-ah fah-MEE-lyah?

28. Make yourself comfortable.
Si accomodi, prego.
see ahk-KAW-mo-dee, PREH-go.

29. I have enjoyed myself very much.
Mi sono divertito molto.
mee SO-no dee-vayr-TEE-toh MOHL-toh.

30. Give my regards to your aunt and uncle.
Mi saluti sua zia e suo zio.
mee sah-LOO-tee SOO-ah TSEE-ah ay SOO-o TSEE-o.

31. Come to see us soon.
Venga a trovarci presto.
VEN-gah ah tro-VAHR-chee PREH-sto.

32. What are you doing tonight?
Che cosa farà stasera?
kay KAW-sah fah-RAH stah-SAY-rah?

33. When may I see you again?
Quando posso rivederla?
KWAHN-doh PAWS- so ree-vay-DAYR-lah?

34. I like you (*fem.*) **very much.**
Lei mi è molto simpatica.
LEH‿ee mee eh MOHL-toh seem-PAH-tee-kah.

35. Give me your address and telephone number.
Mi dia il suo indirizzo e il numero del telefono.
mee DEE-ah eel SOO-o een-dee-REET-tso ay eel NOO- may-ro dayl tay-LEH-fo-no.

36. Congratulations.
Congratulazioni.
kohn-grah-too-lah-TSYOH-nee.

37. Happy birthday.
Buon compleanno.
bwawn kohm-play-AHN-no.

38. Happy New Year.
Buon anno.
bwawn AHN-no.

39. Merry Christmas.
Buon Natale.
bwawn nah-TAH-lay.

YOURSELF

40. My name is John.
Mi chiamo Giovanni.
mee KYAH-mo jo-VAHN-nee.

41. I am thirty-two years old.
Ho trentadue anni.
aw trayn-tah-DOO-ay AHN-nee.

42. I am an American citizen.
Sono cittadino americano.
SO-no cheet-tah-DEE-no ah-may-ree-KAH-no.

43. My mailing address is 920 Broadway.
Il mio recapito è (novecento venti) Broadway.
eel MEE-o ray-KAH-pee-toh eh naw-vay-CHEN-toh VAYN-tee Broadway.

44. I am [a student] (*masc.*).
Sono [uno studente].
SO-no [OO-no stoo-DEN-tay].

45. —— a teacher.
insegnante.
een-say-NYAHN-tay.

46. —— a business man.
commerciante.
kohm-mayr-CHYAHN-tay.

47. I am a friend of Mr. Silvi.
Sono un amico del signor Silvi.
SO-no oon ah-MEE-ko dayl see-NYOHR SEEL-vee.

48. I am here on [business].
Sono qui [per affari].
SO-no kwee [payr ahf-FAH-ree].

49. —— vacation.
in vacanze.
een vah-KAHN-tsay.

50. We are traveling to Bologna.
Andiamo a Bologna.
ahn-DYAH-mo ah bo-LO-nyah.

51. I am [warm].
Ho [caldo].
aw [KAHL-doh].

52. —— cold.
freddo.
FRAYD-doh.

53. —— hungry.
fame.
FAH-may.

54. —— thirsty.
sete.
SAY-tay.

55. I am sorry.
Mi dispiace.
mee dee-SPYAH-chay.

MAKING YOURSELF UNDERSTOOD

56. Do you speak English?
Parla l'inglese?
PAHR-lah leen-GLAY-zay?

57. Does anyone here speak English?
C'è qualcuno qui che parla l'inglese?
cheh kwahl-KOO-no kwee kay PAHR-lah leen-GLAY-zay?

58. I read only English.
Leggo soltanto l'inglese.
LEG-go sohl-TAHN-toh leen-GLAY-zay.

59. I speak a little Italian.
Parlo un po' l'italiano.
PAHR-lo oon paw lee-tah-LYAH-no.

60. Please speak more slowly.
Per favore parli più adagio.
payr fah-VO-ray PAHR-lee pyoo ah-DAH-jo.

61. I (do not) understand.
(Non) capisco.
(nawn) kah-PEE-sko.

62. Do you understand me?
Mi capisce?
mee kah-PEE-shay?

63. I (do not) know.
(Non) so.
(nawn) saw.

64. I (do not) think so.
(Non) mi pare.
(nawn) mee PAH-ray.

65. Repeat it, please.
Lo ripeta, per favore.
lo ree-PEH-tah, payr fah-VO-ray.

66. Write it down, please.
Lo scriva, per favore.
lo SKREE-vah payr fah-VO-ray.

67. What does this word mean?
Che significa questa parola?
kay see-NYEE-fee-kah KWAY-stah pah-RAW-lah?

68. What is that?
Che cos'è?
kay kaw-ZEH?

69. How do you say "pencil" in Italian?
Come si dice "pencil" in italiano?
KO-may see DEE-chay "pencil" een ee-tah-LYAH-no?

GENERAL EXPRESSIONS

70. Yes.
Sì.
see.

71. No.
No.
naw.

72. Perhaps.
Forse.
FOHR-say.

73. Please.
Per favore.
payr fah-VO-ray.

74. Excuse me.
Mi scusi.
mee SKOO-zee.

75. Thanks (very much).
Grazie (tanto).
GRAH-tsyay (TAHN-toh).

76. You are welcome.
Prego.
PREH-go.

77. Very good.
Benissimo.
bay-NEES-see-mo.

78. It is all right.
Va bene.
vah BEH-nay.

79. It doesn't matter.
Non importa.
nawn eem-PAWR-tah.

80. Who are you, please?
Lei chi è, per favore?
LEH‿ee kee eh, payr fah-VO-ray?

81. Who is [that boy]?
Chi è [quel ragazzo]?
kee eh [kwayl rah-GAHT-tso]?

82. —— that girl.
quella ragazza.
KWAYL-lah rah-GAHT-tsah.

83. —— that man.
quell'uomo.
kwayl-LWAW-mo.

84. —— that woman.
quella donna.
KWAYL-lah DAWN-nah.

85. Where is [the men's room]?
Dov'è [il gabinetto per uomini]?
doh-VEH [eel gah-bee-NAYT-toh payr WAW- mee-nee]?

86. —— the ladies' room.
il gabinetto per donne.
eel gah-bee-NAYT-toh payr DAWN-nay.

87. Why?
Perchè?
payr-KEH?

88. Where?
Dove?
DOH-vay?

89. How?
Come?
KO-may?

90. What do you wish?
Che cosa desidera?
kay KAW-sah day-ZEE-day-rah?

91. Come here.
Venga qui.
VEN-gah kwee.

92. Come in.
Avanti.
ah-VAHN-tee.

93. Wait a moment.
Aspetti un momento.
ah-SPET-tee oon mo-MAYN-toh.

94. Not yet.
Non ancora.
nawn ahn-KO-rah.

95. Not now.
Ora no.
O-rah naw.

96. Listen!
Senta!
SEN-tah!

97. Look out!
Attenzione!
aht-ten-TSYOH-nay.

DIFFICULTIES AND REPAIRS

98. Can you [help me]?
Mi potrebbe [aiutare]?
mee po-TREB-bay [ah-yoo-TAH-ray]?

99. —— tell me.
dire.
DEE-ray.

100. I am looking for my friends.
Cerco i miei amici.
CHAYR-ko ee MYEH‿ee ah-MEE-chee.

101. I cannot find my hotel address.
Non riesco a trovare l'indirizzo del mio albergo.
nawn RYEH-sko ah tro-VAH-ray leen-dee-REET-tso dayl MEE-o ahl-BEHR-go.

102. She lost [her purse].
Ha perduto [la borsetta].
ah payr-DOO-toh [lah bohr-SAYT-tah].

103. —— her wallet.
il portafogli.
eel pohr-tah-FAW-lyee.

104. He forgot [his money].
Ha dimenticato [il denaro].
ah dee-mayn-tee-KAH-toh [eel day-NAH-ro].

105. —— his keys.
le chiavi.
lay KYAH-vee.

106. What is the matter?
Cosa c'è?
KAW-zah cheh?

107. I broke my eyeglasses.
Mi si sono rotti gli occhiali.
mee see SO-no ROHT-tee lyee ohk-KYAH-lee.

108. The lost-and-found desk.
L'ufficio degli oggetti smarriti.
loof-FEE-chyoh DAY-lyee ohj-JET-tee zmahr-REE-tee.

109. The police station.
La questura.
lah kway-STOO-rah.

110. I shall call a policeman.
Chiamerò una guardia.
kyah-may-RAW OO-nah GWAHR-dyah.

111. The American consulate.
Il consolato americano.
eel kohn-so-LAH-toh ah-may-ree-KAH-no.

CUSTOMS

112. Where is the customs?
Dov'è la dogana?
doh-VEH la doh-GAH-nah?

113. Here is [my baggage].
Ecco [il mio bagaglio].
EK-ko [eel MEE-o bah-GAH-lyoh].

114. —— my passport.
il mio passaporto.
eel MEE-o pahs-sah-PAWR-toh.

115. —— my identification papers.
le mie carte d'identificazione.
lay MEE-ay KAHR-tay dee-den-tee-fee-kah- TSYOH-nay.

116. —— my health certificate.
il mio certificato medico.
eel MEE-o chayr-tee-fee-KAH-toh MEH-dee-ko.

117. I am in transit.
Sono in transito.
SO-no een TRAHN-see-toh.

118. The bags to your left are mine.
Le valigie alla vostra sinistra sono le mie.
lay vah-LEE-jay AHL-lah VAW-strah see-NEE- strah SO-no lay MEE-ay.

119. I have nothing to declare.
Non ho nulla da dichiarare.
nawn aw NOOL-lah dah dee-kyah-RAH-ray.

120. All this is for my personal use.
Tutto questo è per uso personale.
TOOT-toh KWAY-sto eh payr OO-zo payr-so-NAH- lay.

121. Is it necessary to open everything?
Bisogna aprire tutto?
bee-ZO-nyah ah-PREE-ray TOOT-toh?

122. I cannot open the trunk.
Non riesco ad aprire il baule.
nawn RYEH-sko ahd ah-PREE-ray eel bah-OO-lay.

123. There is nothing here but clothing.
Qui c'è solo del vestiario.
kwee cheh SO-lo dayl vay-STYAH-ryoh.

124. These are gifts.
Questi sono dei regali.
KWAY-stee SO-no day ray-GAH-lee.

125. Must duty be paid on these things?
Su questi oggetti si deve pagare dogana?
soo KWAY-stee ohj-JET-tee see DAY-vay pah-GAH- ray doh-GAH-nah?

126. How much must I pay?
Quanto devo pagare?
KWAHN-toh DAY-vo pah-GAH-ray?

127. This is all I have.
Non ho che questo.
nawn aw kay KWAY-sto.

128. Have you finished?
Ha finito?
ah fee-NEE-toh?

BAGGAGE

129. Where can we check our baggage through to Rome?
Dove possiamo far spedire il bagaglio per Roma?
DOH-vay pohs-SYAH-mo fahr spay-DEE-ray eel bah- GAH-lyoh payr RO-mah?

130. The baggage room.
Il deposito bagagli.
eel day-PAW-zee-toh bah-GAH-lyee.

131. The baggage check.
Lo scontrino.
lo skohn-TREE-no.

132. I want to leave these packages for a few hours.
Vorrei lasciare questi pacchi per qualche ora.
vohr-REH‿ee lah-SHYAH-ray KWAY-stee PAHK-kee payr KWAHL-kay O-rah.

133. Handle this package very carefully.
Stia attento con questo pacco.
STEE-ah aht-TEN-toh kohn KWAY-sto PAHK-ko.

TRAVEL: GENERAL EXPRESSIONS

134. I want to go [to the airline office].
Vorrei andare [all'ufficio delle aviolinee].
vohr-REH‿ee ahn-DAH-ray [ahl-loof-FEE-chyoh DAYL-lay ah-vyoh-LEE-nay-ay].

135. to the travel agent's office.
all'agenzia di viaggi.
ahl-lah-jayn-TSEE-ah dee VYAHJ-jee.

136. How long does it take to go to Sardinia?
Quanto tempo ci vuole per arrivare in Sardegna?
KWAHN-toh TEM-po chee VWAW-lay payr ahr-ree-VAH-ray een sahr-DAY-nyah?

137. When will we arrive at Lake Como?
Quando arriveremo al Lago di Como?
KWAHN-doh ahr-ree-vay-RAY-mo ahl LAH-go dee KAW-mo?

138. Is this the direct way to Naples?
È questa la via più diretta per Napoli?
eh KWAY-stah lah VEE-ah pyoo dee-RET-tah payr NAH-po-lee?

139. Please show me the way [to midtown].
Per favore mi indichi la via per andare [al centro].
payr fah-VO-ray mee EEN-dee-kee lah VEE-ah payr ahn-DAH-ray [ahl CHEN-tro].

140. —— to the shopping district.
al quartiere dei negozi.
ahl kwahr-TYEH-ray DAY nay-GAW-tsee.

141. —— to the residential section.
ai quartieri residenziali.
AH‿ee kwahr-TYEH-ree ray-zee-dayn-TSYAH- lee.

142. —— to the city.
in città.
een cheet-TAH.

143. —— to the village.
al villaggio.
ahl veel-LAHJ-jo.

144. Do I turn [to the north]?
Devo voltare [a nord]?
DAY-vo vohl-TAH-ray [ah nawrd]?

145. —— to the south.
a sud.
ah sood.

146. —— to the east.
a est.
ah est.

147. —— to the west.
a ovest.
ah AW-vayst.

148. —— to the right.
a destra.
ah DEH-strah.

149. —— to the left.
a sinistra.
ah see-NEE-strah.

150. —— after the traffic light.
dopo il semaforo.
DOH-po eel say-MAH-fo-ro.

151. Where is it?
Dov'è?
doh-VEH?

152. This way?
Per di qua?
payr dee kwah?

153. That way?
Per di là?
payr dee lah?

154. Is it [on this side of the street]?
È [da questo lato della strada]?
eh [dah KWAY-stoh LAH-toh DAYL-lah STRAH- dah]?

155. —— on the other side of the street.
dall'altro lato della strada.
dahl-LAHL-tro LAH-toh DAYL-lah STRAH-dah.

156. —— at the corner.
all'angolo.
ahl-LAHN-go-lo.

157. —— in the middle.
in mezzo.
een MED-dzo.

158. —— straight ahead.
a diritto.
ah dee-REET-toh.

159. —— **opposite the park.**
dirimpetto al parco.
dee-reem-PET-toh ahl PAHR-ko.

160. —— **beside the school.**
accanto alla scuola.
ahk-KAHN-toh AHL-lah SKWAW-lah.

161. —— **before the monument.**
davanti al monumento.
dah-VAHN-tee ahl mo-noo-MAYN-toh.

162. —— **behind the building.**
dietro all'edifizio.
DYEH-tro ahl-lay-dee-FEE-tsyoh.

163. —— **forward.**
avanti.
ah-VAHN-tee.

164. —— **back.**
dietro.
DYEH-tro.

165. How far is it?
Quant'è lontano?
kwahn-TEH lohn-TAH-no?

166. Am I going in the right direction?
Vado nella direzione giusta?
VAH-doh NAYL-lah dee-ray-TSYOH-nay JOO-stah?

167. What street is this?
Che strada è questa?
kay STRAH-dah eh KWAY-stah?

TICKETS

168. Where is the ticket window?
Dov'è lo sportello dei biglietti?
doh-VEH lo spohr-TEL-lo day bee-LYAYT-tee?

169. How much is [a round-trip ticket] to Genoa?
Quanto costa [un biglietto di andata e ritorno] per Genova?
KWAHN-toh KAW-stah [oon bee-LYAYT-toh dee ahn-DAH-tah ay ree-TOHR-no] payr JEH-no-vah?

170. —— a one-way ticket.
un biglietto di andata.
oon bee-LYAYT-toh dee ahn-DAH-tah.

171. First class.
Prima classe.
PREE-mah KLAHS-say.

172. Second class.
Seconda classe.
say-KOHN-dah KLAHS-say.

173. Local train.
Treno accelerato.
TREH-no ahch-chay-lay-RAH-toh.

174. Express train.
Direttissimo.
dee-rayt-TEES-see-mo.

175. A reserved seat.
Un posto riservato.
oon PO-sto ree-zayr-VAH-toh.

176. The waiting room.
La sala d'aspetto.
lah SAH-lah dah-SPET-toh.

177. May I stop at Brenta Valley?
Posso sostare in Val di Brenta?
PAWS-so so-STAH-ray een vahl dee BREN-tah?

BOAT

178. When must I go on board?
Quando devo andare a bordo?
KWAHN-doh DAY-vo ahn-DAH-ray ah BOHR-doh?

179. Bon voyage.
Buon viaggio.
bwawn VYAHJ-jo.

180. Where is [the captain]?
Dov'è [il capitano]?
doh-VEH [eel kah-pee-TAH-no]?

181. —— the purser.
il commissario di bordo.
eel kohm-mees-SAH-ryoh dee BOHR-doh.

182. —— the steward.
il cameriere.
eel kah-may-RYEH-ray.

183. The dock.
La banchina.
lah bahn-KEE-nah.

184. The cabin.
La cabina.
lah kah-BEE-nah.

185. The deck.
Il ponte.
eel POHN-tay.

186. The lifeboat.
La scialuppa di salvataggio.
lah shyah-LOOP-pah dee sahl-vah-TAHJ-jo.

187. The life preserver.
Il salvagente.
eel sahl-vah-JEN-tay.

188. I am seasick.
Ho il mal di mare.
aw eel mahl dee MAH-ray.

AIRPLANE

189. Is there taxi service between the hotel and the airport?
C'è servizio di tassì tra l'albergo e l'aeroporto?
cheh sayr-VEE-tsyoh dee tahs-SEE trah lahl-BEHR-go ay lah‿ay-ro-PAWR-toh?

190. At what time will they pick me up?
A che ora mi verranno a prendere?
ah kay O-rah mee vayr-RAHN-no ah PREN-day-ray?

191. Is flight twenty-three on time?
È in orario il volo numero ventitrè?
eh een o-RAH-ryoh eel VO-lo NOO-may-ro vayn-tee-TRAY?

192. How many kilos may I take?
Quanti chili posso portare?
KWAHN-tee KEE-lee PAWS-so pohr-TAH-ray?

193. How much per kilo for excess?
Quanto si paga per il sovrappeso?
KWAHN-toh see PAH-gah payr eel so-vrahp-PAY-zo?

TRAIN

194. Where is the railroad station?
Dov'è la stazione ferroviaria?
doh-VEH lah stah-TSYOH-nay fayr-ro-VYAH-ryah?

195. When does the train for Verona leave?
Quando parte il treno per Verona?
KWAHN-doh PAHR-tay eel TREH-no payr vay-RO-nah?

196. The arrival.
L'arrivo.
lahr-REE-vo.

197. The departure.
La partenza.
lah pahr-TEN-tsah.

198. From what track does the train leave?
Da quale binario parte il treno?
dah KWAH-lay bee-NAH-ryoh PAHR-tay eel TREH-no?

199. Please open the window.
Per favore apra il finestrino.
payr fah-VO-ray AH-prah eel fee-nay-STREE-no.

200. Close the window.
Chiuda il finestrino.
KYOO-dah eel fee-nay-STREE-no.

201. Where is [the diner]?
Dov'è [il vagone ristorante]?
doh-VEH [eel vah-GO-nay ree-stoh-RAHN-tay]?

202. —— the sleeper
il vagon letti.
eel vah-GOHN LET-tee.

203. —— the smoking car.
la vettura per fumatori.
lah vayt-TOO-rah payr foo-mah-TOH-ree.

204. Where are we now?
Dove siamo ora?
DOH-vay SYAH-mo O-rah?

205. May I smoke?
Posso fumare?
PAWS-so foo-MAH-ray?

BUS, STREETCAR AND SUBWAY

206. What streetcar must I take to Popolo Square?
Quale tram devo prendere per andare in Piazza del Popolo?
KWAH-lay trahm DAY-vo PREN-day-ray payr ahn-DAH-ray een PYAHT-tsah dayl PAW-po-lo?

207. The bus stop.
La fermata dell'autobus.
lah fayr-MAH-tah dayl-LAH‿oo-toh-boos.

208. A transfer.
Biglietto di coincidenza.
bee-LYAYT-toh dee ko-een-chee-DEN-tsah.

209. Where is the subway for Piazza Termini?
Dov'è la metropolitana per Piazza Termini?
doh-VEH lah may-tro-po-lee-TAH-nah payr PYAHT- tsah TEHR-mee-nee?

210. Does this bus stop at Nazionale Street?
Si ferma in via Nazionale quest'autobus?
see FAYR-mah een VEE-ah nah-tsyoh-NAH-lay kway- STAH‿oo-toh-boos?

211. Do you go near Italia Avenue?
Passa vicino a Corso d'Italia?
PAHS-sah vee-CHEE-no ah KOHR-so dee-TAH- lyah?

212. Do I have to change?
Devo cambiare?
DAY-vo kahm-BYAH-ray?

213. Driver, please tell me where to get off.
Conduttore, mi dica dove devo scendere.
kohn-doot-TOH-ray, mee DEE-kah DOH-vay DAY-vo SHAYN-day-ray.

214. I want to get off at the next stop, please.
Voglio scendere alla prossima fermata, per favore.
VAW-lyoh SHAYN-day-ray AHL-lah PRAWS-see- mah fayr-MAH-tah, payr fah-VO-ray.

TAXI

215. Please call a taxi for me.
Per favore mi chiami un tassì.
payr fah-VO-ray mee KYAH-mee oon tahs-SEE.

216. Are you free?
È libero?
eh LEE-bay-ro?

217. What do you charge [per hour]?
Quanto prende [all'ora]?
KWAHN-toh PREN-day [ahl-LO-rah]?

218. —— per kilometer.
al chilometro.
ahl kee-LAW-may-tro.

219. Stop here.
Si fermi qui.
see FAYR-mee kwee.

220. Wait for me.
Mi aspetti.
mee ah-SPET-tee.

AUTOMOBILE TRAVEL

221. Where can I rent a car?
Dove posso noleggiare una macchina?
DOH-vay PAWS-so no-layj-JAH-ray OO-nah MAHK-kee-nah?

222. I have an international driver's license.
Ho la patente di guida internazionale.
aw lah pah-TEN-tay dee GWEE-dah een-tayr-nah-tsyoh-NAH-lay.

223. A gas station.
Una stazione di rifornimento.
OO-nah stah-TSYOH-nay dee ree-fohr-nee-MAYN-toh.

224. A garage.
Un' autorimessa.
oon-ah‿oo-toh-ree-MAYS-sah.

225. A mechanic.
Un meccanico.
oon mayk-KAH-nee-ko.

226. Is the road [good]?
La strada è [buona]?
lah STRAH-dah eh [BWAW-nah]?

227. —— bad.
cattiva.
kaht-TEE-vah.

228. Where does that road go?
Dove porta quella strada?
DOH-vay PAWR-tah KWAYL-lah STRAH-dah?

229. What town is [this]?
Che città è [questa]?
kay cheet-TAH eh [KWAY-stah]?

230. —— the next one.
la prossima.
lah PRAWS-see-mah.

231. Can you show it to me on the road map?
Me lo potrebbe indicare sulla carta stradale?
may lo po-TREB-bay een-dee-KAH-ray SOOL-lah KAHR-tah strah-DAH-lay?

232. The tank is [empty].
Il serbatoio è [vuoto].
eel sayr-bah-TOH-yoh eh [VWAW-toh].

233. —— full.
pieno.
PYEH-no.

234. Give me forty liters.
Me ne dia quaranta litri.
may nay DEE-ah kwah-RAHN-tah LEE-tree.

235. Please change the oil.
Per favore, cambi l'olio.
payr fah-VO-ray, KAHM-bee LAW-lyoh.

236. Put water in the battery.
Metta dell'acqua nella batteria.
MAYT-tah dayl-LAHK-kwah NAYL-lah baht-tay-REE-ah.

237. Clean the windshield.
Pulisca il parabrezza.
poo-LEE-skah eel pah-rah-BRAYD-dzah.

238. Will you lubricate the car?
Vuol lubrificare la macchina?
vwawl loo-bree-fee-KAH-ray lah MAHK-kee-nah?

239. Adjust the brakes.
Controlli i freni.
kohn-TRAWL-lee ee FRAY-nee.

240. Will you check the tires?
Vuol verificare le gomme?
vwawl vay-ree-fee-KAH-ray lay GOHM-may?

241. Can you fix [the tire] now?
Può riparare [la gomma] ora?
pwaw ree-pah-RAH-ray [lah GOHM-mah] O-rah?

242. —— a puncture.
una foratura.
OO-nah fo-rah-TOO-rah.

243. The engine overheats.
Il motore riscalda troppo.
eel mo-TOH-ray ree-SKAHL-dah TRAWP-po.

244. The motor [misses].
Il motore [perde dei colpi].
eel mo-TOH-ray [PEHR-day day KOHL-pee].

245. —— stalls.
si spenge.
see SPEN-jay.

246. May I park here for a while?
Posso sostare qui per un poco?
PAWS-so so-STAH-ray kwee payr oon PAW-ko?

HOTEL

247. I am looking for [a good hotel].
Cerco [un buon albergo].
CHAYR-ko [oon bwawn ahl-BEHR-go].

248. —— an inexpensive hotel.
un albergo a un prezzo medio.
oon ahl-BEHR-go ah oon PRET-tso MEH-dyoh.

249. —— a boarding house.
una pensione.
OO-nah payn-SYOH-nay.

250. —— a furnished apartment.
un appartamento ammobigliato.
oon ahp-pahr-tah-MAYN-toh ahm-mo-bee-LYAH- toh.

251. I (do not) want to be [in the center of town].
(Non) vorrei stare [in centro].
(nawn) vohr-REH‿ee STAH-ray [een CHEN-tro].

252. —— where it is not so noisy.
dove non c'è tanto rumore.
DOH-vay nawn cheh TAHN-toh roo-MO-ray.

253. I have a reservation for today.
Ho una prenotazione per oggi.
aw OO-nah pray-no-tah-TSYOH-nay payr AWJ-jee.

254. Do you have [a vacancy]?
Ha [una camera libera]?
ah [OO-nah KAH-may-rah LEE-bay-rah]?

255. —— a single room.
una camera a un letto.
OO-nah KAH-may-rah ah oon LET-toh.

256. —— a double room.
una camera per due.
OO-nah KAH-may-rah payr DOO-ay.

257. —— an air-conditioned room.
una camera con aria condizionata.
OO-nah KAH-may-rah kohn AH-ryah kohn-dee-tsyoh-NAH-tah.

258. —— a suite.
un appartamento.
oon ahp-pahr-tah-MAYN-toh.

259. I want a room [with a double bed].
Vorrei una camera [con letto matrimoniale].
vohr-REH‿ee OO-nah KAH-may-rah [kohn LET-toh mah-tree-mo-NYAH-lay].

260. —— with twin beds.
a due letti.
ah DOO-ay LET-tee.

261. —— with a bath.
con bagno.
kohn BAH-nyoh.

262. —— with a shower.
con doccia.
kohn DOHCH-chyah.

263. I want a room [without meals].
Vorrei una camera [senza pensione].
vohr REH‿ee OO-nah KAH-may-rah [SEN-tsah payn-SYOH-nay].

264. —— for tonight.
per stanotte.
payr stah-NAWT-tay.

265. —— for several days.
per parecchi giorni.
payr pah-REK-kee JOHR-nee.

266. —— for two persons.
per due persone.
payr DOO-ay payr-SO-nay.

267. I should like to see the room.
Vorrei vedere la camera.
vohr-REH‿ee vay-DAY-ray lah KAH-may-rah.

268. Is it [upstairs]?
È di [sopra]?
eh dee [SO-prah]?

269. —— downstairs.
di sotto.
dee SOHT-toh.

270. Is there an elevator?
C'è l'ascensore?
cheh lah-shayn-SO-ray?

271. Room service, please.
Servizio, per favore.
sayr-VEE-tsyoh, payr fah-VO-ray.

272. Please send [a porter] to my room soon.
Per favore tra poco mi mandi [un cameriere].
payr fah-VO-ray trah PAW-ko mee MAHN-dee [oon kah-may-RYEH-ray].

273. —— a chambermaid.
una cameriera.
OO-nah kah-may-RYEH-rah.

274. —— a bellhop.
il "piccolo."
eel PEEK-ko-lo.

275. Please call me at a quarter past nine o'clock.
Per favore mi chiami alle nove e un quarto.
payr fah-VO-ray mee KYAH-mee AHL-lay NAW- vay ay oon KWAHR-toh.

276. I do not want to be disturbed until then.
Non voglio essere disturbato prima di allora.
nawn VAW-lyoh ES-say-ray dee-stoor-BAH-toh PREE- mah dee ahl-LO-rah.

277. We should like to have breakfast in my room.
Vorremmo fare colazione in camera.
vohr-RAYM-mo FAH-ray ko-lah-TSYOH-nay een KAH-may-rah.

278. Who is it?
Chi è?
kee eh?

279. Come back later.
Ritorni più tardi.
ree-TOHR-nee pyoo TAHR-dee.

280. I need [a blanket].
Ho bisogno di [una coperta].
aw bee-ZO-nyoh dee [OO nah ko-PEHR-tah].

281. —— a pillow.
un cuscino.
oon koo-SHEE-no.

282. —— a pillowcase.
una federa.
OO-nah FEH-day-rah.

283. —— coat hangers.
grucce.
GROOCH-chay.

284. —— sheets.
lenzuola.
layn-TSWAW-lah.

285. —— soap.
sapone.
sah-PO-nay.

286. —— towels.
asciugamani.
ah-shyoo-gah-MAH-nee.

287. —— a bath mat.
uno scendibagno.
OO-no shayn-dee-BAH-nyoh.

288. —— toilet paper.
carta igienica.
KAHR-tah ee-JYEH-nee-kah.

289. I should like to speak to the manager.
Vorrei parlare al direttore.
vohr-REH‿ee pahr-LAH-ray ahl dee-rayt-TOH-ray.

290. My room key, please.
La chiave della mia camera, per favore.
lah KYAH-vay DAYL-lah MEE-ah KAH-may-rah, payr fah-VO-ray.

291. Are there any letters or messages for me?
Ci sono lettere o messaggi per me?
chee SO-no LET-tay-ray o mays-SAHJ-jee payr may?

292. What is my room number?
Qual'è il numero della mia camera?
kwah-LEH eel NOO-may-ro DAYL-lah MEE-ah KAH-may-rah?

293. I am leaving at 10 o'clock.
Parto alle dieci.
PAHR-toh AHL-lay DYEH-chee.

294. Please make out my bill.
Per favore mi prepari il conto.
payr fah-VO-ray mee pray-PAH-ree eel KOHN-toh.

295. Are the service charge and tax included?
Il servizio e le tasse sono inclusi?
eel sayr-VEE-tsyoh ay lay TAHS-say SO-no een- KLOO-zee?

296. Forward my mail to American Express in Rome.
Faccia proseguire la mia posta all'American Express a Roma.
FAHCH-chyah pro-say-GWEE-ray lah MEE-ah PAW-stah ahl AMERICAN EXPRESS ah RO-mah.

AT THE CAFÉ

297. Bartender, I'd like to have [a drink].
Barista, vorrei [una bibita].
bah-REE-stah, vohr-REH‿ee [OO-nah BEE-bee-tah].

298. —— a bottle of mineral water.
una bottiglia d'acqua minerale.
OO-nah boht-TEE-lyah DAHK-kwah mee-nay-RAH-lay.

299. —— a glass of sherry.
un bicchiere di sherry.
oon beek-KYEH-ray dee "sherry."

300. —— some champagne.
dello spumante.
DAYL-lo spoo-MAHN-tay.

301. —— some [light] dark beer.
della birra [chiara] scura.
DAYL-lah BEER-rah [KYAH-rah] SKOO-rah.

302. —— some [red] white wine.
del vino [rosso] bianco.
dayl VEE-no [ROHS-so] BYAHN-ko.

303. Let's have another.
Prendiamone un altro.
pren-DYAH-mo-nay oon AHL-tro.

304. To your health!
Alla salute!
AHL-lah sah-LOO-tay!

AT THE RESTAURANT

305. Can you recommend a restaurant [for dinner]?
Mi potrebbe raccomandare un ristorante [per il pranzo]?
mee po-TREB-bay rahk-ko-mahn-DAH-ray oon ree-stoh-RAHN-tay [payr eel PRAHN-dzo]?

306. —— for breakfast.
per la prima colazione.
payr lah PREE-mah ko-lah-TSYOH-nay.

307. —— for lunch.
per la colazione.
payr lah ko-lah-TSYOH-nay.

308. At what time is supper served?
A che ora si va a cena?
ah kay O-rah see vah ah CHAY-nah?

309. Are you [my waiter]?
Lei è [il mio cameriere]?
LEH‿ee eh [eel MEE-o kah-may-RYEH-ray]?

310. —— my waitress.
la mia cameriera.
lah MEE-ah kah-may-RYEH-rah.

311. Give me a table for two near the window, if possible.
Mi dia una tavola per due persone vicino alla finestra, se possibile.
mee DEE-ah OO-nah TAH-vo-lah payr DOO-ay payr-SO-nay vee-CHEE-no AHL-lah fee-NEH- strah, say pohs-SEE-bee-lay.

312. We want to dine [à la carte].
Vogliamo mangiare [alla carta].
vo-LYAH-mo mahn-JAH-ray [AHL-lah KAHR-tah].

313. —— table d'hôte.
a prezzo fisso.
ah PRET-tso FEES-so.

314. Bring me [the menu].
Mi porti [la lista].
mee PAWR-tee [lah LEE-stah].

315. —— the wine list.
la lista dei vini.
lah LEE-stah day VEE-nee.

316. —— a napkin.
un tovagliolo.
oon toh-vah-LYAW-lo.

317. —— a fork.
una forchetta.
OO-nah fohr-KAYT-tah.

318. —— a knife.
un coltello.
oon kohl-TEL-lo.

319. —— a plate.
un piatto.
oon PYAHT-toh.

320. —— a teaspoon.
un cucchiaino.
oon kook-kyah-EE-no.

321. —— a large spoon.
un cucchiaio.
oon kook-KYAH-yoh.

322. I want something [simple].
Voglio qualche cosa [di semplice].
VAW-lyoh KWAHL-kay KAW-zah [dee SAYM-plee-chay].

323. —— not too spicy.
di non troppo piccante.
dee nawn TRAWP-po peek-KAHN-tay.

324. —— not too sweet.
di non troppo dolce.
dee nawn TRAWP-po DOHL-chay.

325. —— not too fat.
di non troppo grasso.
dee nawn TRAWP-po GRAHS-so.

326. —— fried.
di fritto.
dee FREET-toh.

327. —— boiled.
di bollito.
dee bohl-LEE-toh.

328. I like the meat [rare].
Mi piace la carne [al sangue].
mee PYAH-chay lah KAHR-nay [ahl SAHN-gway].

329. —— medium.
non troppo cotta.
nawn TRAWP-po KAWT-tah.

330. —— well done.
ben cotta.
ben KAWT-tah.

331. A little more.
Un po' di più.
oon paw dee pyoo.

332. A little less.
Un po' di meno.
oon paw dee MAY-no.

333. Enough.
Basta.
BAH-stah.

334. I did not order this.
Non ho ordinato questo.
nawn aw ohr-dee-NAH-toh KWAY-stoh.

335. May I change this for a salad?
Posso cambiare questo con un insalata?
PAWS-so kahm-BYAH-ray KWAY-stoh kohn oon een-sah-LAH-tah?

336. The check, please.
Il conto, per favore.
eel KOHN-toh, payr fah-VO-ray.

337. Is the tip included?
La mancia è inclusa?
lah MAHN-chyah eh een-KLOO-zah?

338. There is a mistake in the bill.
C'è uno sbaglio nel conto.
cheh OO-no ZBAH-lyoh nayl KOHN-toh.

339. What are these charges for?
Questo per che cos'è?
KWAY-sto payr kay kaw-ZEH?

340. Keep the change.
Tenga il resto.
TEN-gah eel REH-sto.

341. The food and service were excellent.
Il cibo e il servizio sono stati eccellenti.
eel CHEE-bo ay eel sayr-VEE-tsyoh SO-no STAH-tee aych-chayl-LEN-tee.

342. Hearty appetite!
Buon appetito!
bwawn ahp-pay-TEE-toh!

FOOD LIST

343. Please bring me some drinking water [with- out ice].
Per favore mi porti dell'acqua da bere [senza ghiaccio].
payr fah-VO-ray mee PAWR-tee dayl-LAHK-kwah dah BAY-ray [SEN-tsah GYAHCH-chyoh].

344. —— with ice.
con ghiaccio.
kohn GYAHCH-chyoh.

345. The bread. Il pane.
eel PAH-nay.

346. The butter. Il burro. *eel BOOR-ro.*

347. The garlic. L'aglio. *LAH-lyoh.*

348. The mustard. La senapa. *lah SEH-nah-pah.*

349. The oil. L'olio. *LAW-lyoh.*

350. The pepper. Il pepe. *eel PAY-pay.*

351. The salt. Il sale. *eel SAH-lay.*

352. The sauce. Il sugo. *eel SOO-go.*

353. The sugar. Lo zucchero. *lo DZOOK-kay-ro.*

354. The vinegar. L'aceto. *lah-CHAY-toh.*

BREAKFAST FOODS

355. May I have [some fruit juice]?
Potrei avere [del succo di frutta]?
po-TREH‿ee ah-VAY-ray [dayl SOOK-ko dee FROOT-tah]?

356. —— some orange juice. del succo d'arancio.
dayl SOOK-ko dah-RAHN-chyoh.

357. —— **some tomato juice.**
del succo di pomodoro.
dayl SOOK-ko dee po-mo-DAW-ro.

358. —— **some stewed prunes.** delle prugne cotte.
DAYL-lay PROO-nyay KAWT-tay.

359. —— **some cooked cereal.** del cereale cotto.
dayl chay-ray-AH-lay KAWT-toh.

360. —— **some toast and jam.**
del pane tostato e marmellata.
dayl PAH-nay toh-STAH-toh ay mahr-mayl-LAH-tah.

361. —— **some rolls.** dei panini. *day pah-NEE-nee.*

362. —— **an omelette.** una frittata.
OO-nah freet-TAH-tah.

363. —— **some soft-boiled eggs.**
delle uova à la coque.
DAYL-lay WAW-vah ah lah kohk.

364. —— **some medium-boiled eggs.**
delle uova bazzotte.
DAYL-lay WAW-vah bahd-DZAWT-tay.

365. —— **some hard-boiled eggs.** delle uova sode.
DAYL-lay WAW-vah SAW-day.

366. —— **some fried eggs.** delle uova fritte.
DAYL-lay WAW-vah FREET-tay.

367. —— **some scrambled eggs.**
delle uova strapazzate.
DAYL-lay WAW-vah strah-paht-TSAH-tay.

368. —— **some bacon and eggs.**
delle uova col "bacon."
DAYL-lay WAW-vah kohl "bacon."

369. —— some ham and eggs.
delle uova al prosciutto.
DAYL-lay WAW-vah ahl pro-SHOOT-toh.

SOUPS AND ENTRÉES

370. I want [some chicken soup].
Vorrei [del brodo di pollo].
vohr-REH‿ee [dayl BRAW-doh dee POHL-lo].

371. —— some vegetable soup.
della minestra di verdura.
DAYL-lah mee-NES-trah dee vehr-DOO-rah.

372. —— some anchovies. delle acciughe.
DAYL-lay ahch-CHYOO-gay.

373. —— some beef. del manzo. *dayl MAHN-dzo.*

374. —— some roast beef. del roastbeef.
dayl "roastbeef."

375. —— some [broiled] fried chicken.
del pollo [allo spiedo] fritto.
dayl POHL-lo [AHL-lo SPYEH-doh] FREET-toh.

376. —— some roast chicken. del pollo arrosto.
dayl POHL-lo ahr-RAW-sto.

377. —— some duck. dell'anitra.
dayl-LAH-nee-trah.

378. —— some fish. del pesce. *dayl PAY-shay.*

379. —— some goose. dell'oca. *dayl-LAW-kah.*

380. —— some lamb. dell'agnello.
dayl-lah-NYEL-lo.

381. —— some liver. del fegato. *dayl FAY-gah-toh.*

382. —— **some lobster.** dell'aragosta.
dayl-lah-rah-GO-stah.

383. —— **some oysters.** delle ostriche.
DAYL-lay AW-stree-kay.

384. —— **some pork.** del maiale.
dayl mah-YAH-lay.

385. —— **some sardines.** delle sardine.
DAYL-lay sahr-DEE-nay.

386. —— **some sausage.** delle salsicce.
DAYL-lay sahl-SEECH-chay.

387. —— **some shrimps.** dei gamberi.
day GAHM-bay-ree.

388. —— **some steak.** una bistecca.
OO-nah bee-STEK-kah.

389. —— **some veal.** del vitello. *dayl vee-TEL-lo.*

VEGETABLES AND SALAD

390. **I want [some asparagus].**
Vorrei [degli asparagi].
vohr-REH‿ee [DAY-lyee ah-SPAH-rah-jee].

391. —— **some beans.** dei fagioli.
day fah-JAW-lee.

392. —— **some cabbage.** del cavolo.
dayl KAH-vo-lo.

393. —— **some carrots.** delle carote.
DAYL-lay kah-RAW-tay.

394. —— **some cauliflower.** del cavolfiore.
dayl kah-vohl-FYOH-ray.

395. —— **some celery and olives.**
del sedano e delle olive.
dayl SEH-dah-no ay DAYL-lay o-LEE-vay.

396. —— **some cucumber.** dei cetrioli.
day chay-tree-AW-lee.

397. —— **some lettuce.** della lattuga.
DAYL-lah laht-TOO-gah.

398. —— **some mushrooms.** dei funghi.
day FOON-gee.

399. —— **some onions.** delle cipolle.
DAYL-lay chee-POHL-lay.

400. —— **some peas.** dei piselli.
day pee-ZEL-lee.

401. —— **some peppers.** dei peperoni.
day pay-pay-RO-nee.

402. —— **some boiled potatoes.**
delle patate bollite.
DAYL-lay pah-TAH-tay bohl-LEE-tay.

403. —— **some mashed potatoes.**
del purè di patate.
dayl poo-REH dee pah-TAH-tay.

404. —— **some baked potatoes.**
delle patate al forno.
DAYL-lay pah-TAH-tay ahl FOHR-no.

405. —— **some fried potatoes.** delle patate fritte.
DAYL-lay pah-TAH-tay FREET-tay.

406. —— **some rice.** del riso. *dayl REE-zo.*

407. —— **some spinach.** degli spinaci.
DAY-lyee spee-NAH-chee.

408. —— **some tomatoes.** dei pomodori.
day po-mo-DAW-ree.

FRUITS

409. Do you have [an apple]?
Ha [una mela]?
ah [OO-nah MAY-lah]?

410. —— **some cherries.** delle ciliege.
DAYL-lay chee-LYEH-jay.

411. —— **half a grapefruit.** mezzo pompelmo.
MED-dzo pohm-PEL-mo.

412. —— **some grapes.** dell'uva. *dayl-LOO-vah.*

413. —— **a lemon.** un limone. *oon lee-MO-nay.*

414. —— **some melon.** del melone.
dayl may-LO-nay.

415. —— **an orange.** un arancio.
oon ah-RAHN-chyoh.

416. —— **a peach.** una pesca. *OO-nah PEH-skah.*

417. —— **some raspberries.** dei lamponi.
day lahm-PO-nee.

418. —— **some strawberries.** delle fragole.
DAYL-lay FRAH-go-lay.

BEVERAGES

419. A cup of black coffee.
Una tazza di caffè nero.
OO-nah TAHT-tsah dee kahf-FEH NAY-ro.

420. Coffee with milk. Caffè e latte.
kahf-FEH ay LAHT-tay.

421. A glass of milk. Un bicchiere di latte.
oon beek-KYEH-ray dee LAHT-tay.

422. Some tea. Del tè. *dayl teh.*

423. Some lemonade. Della limonata.
DAYL-lah lee-mo-NAH-tah.

DESSERTS

424. I should like to have [some cake].
Vorrei avere [del dolce].
vohr-REH‿ee ah-VAY-ray [dayl DOHL-chay].

425. —— a piece of pie. una fetta di torta di frutta.
OO-nah FAYT-tah dee TOHR-tah de FROOT- tah.

426. —— some cheese. del formaggio.
dayl fohr-MAHJ-jo.

427. —— some cookies. dei biscotti.
day bee-SKAWT-tee.

428. —— some custard. della crema.
DAYL-lah KREH-mah.

429. —— some chocolate ice cream.
del gelato di cioccolata.
dayl jay-LAH-toh dee chyohk-ko-LAH-tah.

430. —— some vanilla ice cream.
del gelato alla vaniglia.
dayl jay-LAH-toh AHL-lah vah-NEE-lyah.

CHURCH

431. Is there an English-speaking [priest]?
C'è un [prete] che parla l'inglese?
cheh oon [PREH-tay] kay PAHR-lah leen-GLAY-zay?

432. —— rabbi.
rabbino.
rahb-BEE-no.

433. —— minister.
pastore protestante.
pah-STOH-ray pro-tay-STAHN-tay.

434. A [Catholic] church.
Una chiesa [cattolica].
OO-nah KYEH-zah [kaht-TAW-lee-kah].

435. —— Protestant.
protestante.
pro-tay-STAHN-tay.

436. A synagogue.
Una sinagoga.
OO-nah see-nah-GO-gah.

437. When is the [service]?
A che ora è la [funzione]?
ah kay O-rah eh lah [foon-TSYOH-nay]?

438. —— mass.
la messa.
lah MAYS-sah.

SIGHTSEEING

439. We want a licensed guide who speaks English.
Vorremmo una guida patentata che parli l'inglese.
vohr-RAYM-mo OO-nah GWEE-dah pah-ten-TAH- tah kay pahr-lee leen-GLAY-zay.

440. What is the charge [per hour]?
Quanto si paga [all'ora]?
KWAHN-toh see PAH-gah [ahl-LO-rah]?

441. —— **per day.**
al giorno.
ahl JOHR-no.

442. **I am interested [in architecture].**
Mi interesso [di architettura].
mee een-tay-RES-so [dee ahr-kee-tayt-TOO-rah].

443. —— **in painting.**
di pittura.
dee peet-TOO-rah.

444. —— **in sculpture.**
di scultura.
dee skool-TOO-rah.

445. **Show us [the most important sights].**
Ci mostri [le cose più interessanti].
chee MO-stree [lay KAW-zay pyoo een-tay-rays-SAHN-tee].

446. —— **the castle.**
il castello.
eel kah-STEL-lo.

447. —— **the museum.**
il museo.
eel moo-ZEH-o.

448. **When does it [open]?**
Quando [apre]?
KWAHN-doh [AH-pray]?

449. —— **close.**
chiude.
KYOO-day.

450. **Where is [the entrance]?**
Dov'è [l'entrata]?
doh-VEH [layn-TRAH-tah]?

451. —— **the exit.**
l'uscita.
loo-SHEE-tah.

AMUSEMENTS

452. **I should like to go [to a concert].**
Mi piacerebbe andare [ad un concerto].
mee pyah-chay-REB-bay ahn-DAH-ray [ahd oon kohn-CHEHR-toh].

453. —— **to a matinee.**
a una rappresentazione diurna.
ah OO-nah rahp-pray-zayn-tah-TSYOH-nay DYOOR-nah.

454. —— **to the movies.**
al cinematografo.
ahl chee-nay-mah-TAW-grah-fo.

455. —— to a night club.
a un cabaret.
ah oon kah-bah-RAY.

456. —— to the opera.
all'opera.
ahl-LAW-pay-rah.

457. —— to the theatre.
a teatro.
ah tay-AH-tro.

458. —— to the box office.
al botteghino.
ahl boht-tay-GEE-no.

459. What is playing tonight?
Stasera che cosa danno?
stah-SAY-rah kay KAW-zah DAHN-no?

460. When will [the evening performance] start?
Quando comincerà [lo spettacolo serale]?
KWAHN-doh ko-meen-chyah-RAH [lo spet-TAH-ko-lo say-RAH-lay]?

461. Have you [a balcony seat] for tonight?
Ha [un posto in galleria] per stasera?
ah [oon PO-sto een gahl-lay-REE-ah] payr stah-SAY-rah?

462. —— any orchestra seats.
delle poltrone di platea.
DAYL-lay pohl-TRO-nay dee plah-TEH-ah.

463. —— a box.
un palco.
oon PAHL-ko.

464. Can I see well from there?
Si può veder bene di là?
see pwaw vay-DAYR BEH-nay dee lah?

465. Where can we go to dance?
Dove si può andare a ballare?
DOH-vay see pwaw ahn-DAH-ray ah bahl-LAH-ray?

466. May I have this dance?
Posso invitarla per questa danza?
PAWS-so een-vee-TAHR-lah payr KWAY-stah DAHN-tsah?

SPORTS

467. Let's go [to the beach].
Andiamo [alla spiaggia].
ahn-DYAH-mo [AHL-lah SPYAHJ-jah].

468.—— to the horse races.
alle corse dei cavalli.
AHL-lay KOHR-say day kah-VAHL-lee.

469.—— to the swimming pool.
alla piscina.
AHL-lah pee-SHEE-nah.

470.—— to the stadium.
allo stadio.
AHL-lo STAH-dyoh.

471. I'd like to play [tennis].
Mi piacerebbe giocare al [tennis].
mee pyah-chay-REB-bay jo-KAH-ray ahl [TEN- nees].

472.—— golf.
golf.
gawlf.

473. Can we go [fishing]?
Possiamo andare [a pescare]?
pohs-SYAH-mo ahn-DAH-ray [ah pay-SKAH-ray]?

474.—— horseback riding.
a cavallo.
ah kah-VAHL-lo.

475. —— skating.
a pattinare.
ah paht-tee-NAH-ray.

476. —— skiing.
a sciare.
ah shee-AH-ray.

477. —— swimming.
a nuotare.
ah nwaw-TAH-ray.

BANK AND MONEY

478. Where can I get dollars changed?
Dove posso cambiare dei dollari?
DOH-vay PAWS-so kahm-BYAH-ray day DAWL- lah-ree?

479. Where is the nearest bank?
Dov'è la banca più vicina?
doh-VEH lah BAHN-kah pyoo vee-CHEE-nah?

480. Will the bank cash [a personal check]?
Mi cambieranno [un assegno personale] alla banca?
mee kahm-byay-RAHN-no [oon ahs-SAY-nyoh payr-so-NAH-lay] AHL-lah BAHN-kah?

481. —— a traveler's check.
un traveler chèque.
oon "traveler check."

482. What is the exchange rate on the dollar?
Qual'è il cambio del dollaro?
kwah-LEH eel KAHM-byoh dayl DAWL-lah-ro?

483. Can you change fifty dollars into lire?
Mi può cambiare cinquanta dollari in lire?
mee pwaw kahm-BYAH-ray cheen-KWAHN-tah DAWL-lah-ree een LEE-ray?

484. May I have [some large bills]?
Posso avere [delle banconote di grosso taglio]?
PAWS-so ah-VAY-ray [DAYL-lay bahn-ko-NO-tay dee GRAWS-so TAH-lyoh]?

485. —— some small bills.
delle banconote di piccolo taglio.
DAYL-lay bahn-ko-NO-tay dee PEEK-ko-lo TAH-lyoh.

486. —— some small change.
degli spiccioli.
DAY-lyee SPEECH-chyoh-lee.

SHOPPING

487. I want to go shopping.
Vorrei andare a fare delle spese.
vohr-REH‿ee ahn-DAH-ray ah FAH-ray DAYL-lay SPAY-zay.

488. I (do not) like this one.
(Non) mi piace questo qui.
(nawn) mee PYAH-chay KWAY-sto kwee.

489. How much is it?
Quanto costa?
KWAHN-toh KAW-stah?

490. The price is 1,500 lire.
Il prezzo è mille cinquecento lire.
eel PRET-tso eh MEEL-lay cheen-kway-CHEN-toh LEE-ray.

491. I prefer something [better].
Preferirei qualche cosa [di migliore].
pray-fay-ree-REH‿ee KWAHL-kay KAW-zah [dee mee-LYOH-ray].

492. —— cheaper.
di meno caro.
dee MAY-no KAH-ro.

493. —— larger.
di più grande.
dee pyoo GRAHN-day.

494. —— smaller.
di più piccolo.
dee pyoo PEEK-ko-lo.

495. —— stronger.
di più forte.
dee pyoo FAWR-tay.

496. May I try this on?
Lo posso provare?
lo PAWS-so pro-VAH-ray?

497. Can I order size 32?
Posso ordinare il trentadue?
PAWS-so ohr-dee-NAH-ray eel trayn-tah-DOO-ay?

498. Please take [the measurements].
Per favore prenda [le misure].
payr fah-VO-ray PREN-dah [lay mee-ZOO-ray].

499. —— the length.
la lunghezza.
lah loon-GET-tsah.

500. —— the width.
la larghezza.
lah lahr-GAYT-tsah.

501. How long will it take to make?
Quanto ci vorrà per la confezione?
KWAHN-toh chee vohr-RAH payr lah kohn-fay-TSYOH-nay?

502. I'll return later.
Ripasserò più tardi.
ree-pahs-say-RAW pyoo TAHR-dee.

503. Can you ship it to New York City?
Lo può spedire a New York?
lo pwaw spay-DEE-ray ah New York?

504. Do I pay [the salesgirl]?
Pago [alla commessa]?
PAH-go [AHL-lah kohm-MAYS-sah]?

505. —— the salesman.
al commesso.
ahl kohm-MAYS-so.

506. —— the cashier.
al cassiere.
ahl kahs-SYEH-ray.

507. Please bill me.
Per favore mi mandi il conto.
payr fah-VO-ray mee MAHN-dee eel KOHN-toh.

CLOTHING

508. I want to buy [a bathing cap].
Vorrei comprare [una cuffia da bagno].
vohr-REH‿ee kohm-PRAH-ray [OO-nah KOOF-fyah dah BAH-nyoh].

509. —— a bathing suit. un costume da bagno.
oon ko-STOO-may dah BAH-nyoh.

510. —— a blouse. una camicetta.
OO-nah kah-mee-CHAYT-tah.

511. —— a brassiere. un reggipetto.
oon rayj-jee-PET-toh.

512. —— a coat. un mantello. *oon mahn-TEL-lo.*

513. —— a dress. un vestito. *oon vay-STEE-toh.*

514. —— a pair of gloves. un paio di guanti.
oon PAH-yoh dee GWAHN-tee.

515.—— **a handbag.** una borsetta.
OO-nah bohr-SAYT-tah.

516.—— **one dozen handkerchiefs.**
una dozzina di fazzoletti.
OO-nah dod-DZEE-nah dee faht-tso-LAYT-tee.

517.—— **a hat.** un cappello. *oon kahp-PEL-lo.*

518.—— **a jacket.** una giacca. *OO-nah JAHK-kah.*

519.—— **some lingerie.** della biancheria.
DAYL-lah byahn-kay-REE-ah.

520.—— **a nightgown.** una camicia da notte.
OO-nah kah-MEE-chyah dah NAWT-tay.

521.—— **a raincoat.** un impermeabile.
oon eem-payr-may‿AH-bee-lay.

522.—— **a pair of shoes.** un paio di scarpe.
oon PAH-yoh dee SKAHR-pay.

523.—— **some shoelaces.** dei lacci per le scarpe.
day LAHCH-chee payr lay SKAHR-pay.

524.—— **a skirt.** una gonna. *OO-nah GOHN-nah.*

525.—— **a pair of slippers.** un paio di pantofole.
oon PAH-yoh dee pahn-TAW-fo-lay.

526.—— **a pair of socks.** un paio di calzini.
oon PAH-yoh dee kahl-TSEE-nee.

527.—— **a pair of nylon stockings.**
un paio di calze di nailon.
oon PAH-yoh dee KAHL-tsay dee "nylon."

528.—— **a suit.** un tailleur. *oon tah-YEHR.*

529. —— **a woolen sweater.** un golf di lana.
oon gawlf dee LAH-nah.

530. —— **some neckties.** delle cravatte.
DAYL-lay krah-VAHT-tay.

531. —— **a pair of trousers.** un paio di calzoni.
oon PAH-yoh dee kahl-TSO-nee.

532. —— **some underwear.**
della biancheria personale.
DAYL-lah byahn-kay-REE-ah payr-so-NAH- lay.

MISCELLANEOUS

533. Do you have [ashtrays]?
Ha [dei portacenere]?
ah [day pohr-tah-CHAY-nay-ray]?

534. —— **artists' supplies.** articoli per pittori.
ahr-TEE-ko-lee payr peet-TOH-ree.

535. —— **a box of chocolate candy.**
una scatola di cioccolatini.
OO-nah SKAH-toh-lah dee chyohk-ko-lah-TEE- nee.

536. —— **some china.** delle stoviglie di porcellana.
DAYL-lay stoh-VEE-lyay dee pohr-chayl-LAH- nah.

537. —— **a silver compact.** un portacipria d'argento.
oon pohr-tah-CHEE-pryah dahr-JEN-toh.

538. —— **some gold cuff links.** dei gemelli d'oro.
day jay-MEL-lee DAW-ro.

539. —— **some dolls.** delle bambole.
DAYL-lay BAHM-bo-lay.

540. —— **some earrings.** degli orecchini.
DAY-lyee o-rayk-KEE-nee.

541. —— **musical instruments.**
strumenti musicali.
stroo-MAYN-tee moo-zee-KAH-lee.

542. —— **some perfume.** del profumo.
dayl pro-FOO-mo.

543. —— **some pictures.** dei quadri.
day KWAH-dree.

544. —— **a radio.** una radio. *OO-nah RAH-dyoh.*

545. —— **some records.** dei dischi. *day DEE-skee.*

546. —— **some silverware.** dell'argenteria.
dayl-lahr-jayn-tay-REE-ah.

547. —— **some souvenirs of Rome.**
dei ricordi di Roma.
DEH-ee ree-KAWR-dee dee RO-mah.

548. —— **some toys.** dei giocattoli.
day jo-KAHT-toh-lee.

549. —— **a wristwatch.** un orologio da polso.
oon o-ro-LAW-jo dah POHL-so.

COLORS

550. **I want [a lighter shade].**
Voglio [un colore più chiaro].
VAW-lyoh [oon ko-LO-ray pyoo KYAH-ro].

551. —— **a darker shade.** un colore più scuro.
oon ko-LO-ray pyoo SKOO-ro.

552. **Do you have it in [black]?** Ce l'ha in [nero]?
chay lah een [NAY-ro]?

553. —— **blue.** azzurro. *ahd-DZOO-ro.*

554. —— **brown.** marrone. *mahr-RO-nay.*

555. —— **gray.** grigio. *GREE-jo.*

556. —— **green.** verde. *VAYR-day.*

557. —— **orange.** arancione. *ah-rahn-CHYOH-nay.*

558. —— **pink.** rosa. *RAW-zah.*

559. —— **purple.** violetto. *vyoh-LAYT-toh.*

560. —— **red.** rosso. *ROHS-so.*

561. —— **white.** bianco. *BYAHN-ko.*

562. —— **yellow.** giallo. *JAHL-lo.*

STORES

563. Where can I find a bakery?
Dove posso trovare una panetteria?
DOH-vay PAWS-so tro-VAH-ray OO-nah pah-nayt- tay-REE-ah?

564. —— **a candy store.**
una confetteria.
OO-nah kohn-fet-tay-REE-ah.

565. —— **a cigar store.**
un tabaccaio.
oon tah-bahk-KAH-yoh.

566. —— **a clothing store.**
un negozio di vestiario.
oon nay-GAW-tsyoh dee vay-STYAH-ryoh.

567. —— **a department store.**
un magazzino.
oon mah-gahd-DZEE-no.

568. —— **a drugstore.**
una farmacia.
OO-nah fahr-mah-CHEE-ah.

569. —— **a grocery.**
un negozio di generi alimentari.
oon nay-GAW-tsyoh dee JEH-nay-ree ah-lee- mayn-TAH-ree.

570. —— **a hardware store.**
un negozio di articoli casalinghi.
oon nay-GAW-tsyoh dee ahr-TEE-ko-lee kah-zah-LEEN-gee.

571. —— **a hat shop**
una cappelleria.
OO-nah kahp-payl-lay-REE-ah.

572. —— **a milliner.**
una modisteria.
OO-nah mo-dee-stay-REE-ah.

573. —— **a jewelry store.**
una gioielleria.
OO-nah jo-yayl-lay-REE-ah.

574. —— **a market.**
un mercato.
oon mayr-KAH-toh.

575. —— **a meat market.**
una macelleria.
OO-nah mah-chayl-lay-REE-ah.

576. —— **a pastry shop.**
una pasticceria.
OO-nah pah-steech-chay-REE-ah.

577. —— **a shoemaker.**
un calzolaio.
oon kahl-tso-LAH-yoh.

578. —— **a shoe store.**
una calzoleria.
OO-nah kahl-tso-lay-REE-ah.

579. —— **a tailor shop.**
una sartoria.
OO-nah sahr-toh-REE-ah.

580. —— **a watchmaker.**
un orologiaio.
oon o-ro-lo-JAH-yoh.

BOOKSTORE AND STATIONER'S

581. Where is [a bookstore]?
Dov'è [una libreria]?
doh-VEH [OO-nah lee-bray-REE-ah]?

582. —— **a news dealer.**
un giornalaio.
oon johr-nah-LAH-yoh.

583. —— **a stationer's.**
un cartolaio.
oon kahr-toh-LAH-yoh.

584. I want to buy [a book].
Vorrei comprare [un libro].
vohr-REH‿ee kohm-PRAH-ray [oon LEE-bro].

585. —— a guidebook.
una guida.
OO-nah GWEE-dah.

586. —— a dictionary.
un dizionario.
oon dee-tsyoh-NAH-ryoh.

587. —— a magazine.
una rivista.
OO-nah ree-VEE-stah.

588. —— a map of Italy.
una carta geografica dell'Italia.
OO-nah KAHR-tah jay-o-GRAH-fee-kah dayl- lee-TAH-lyah.

589. —— a newspaper.
un giornale.
oon johr-NAH-lay.

590. I should like [some envelopes].
Vorrei [delle buste].
vohr-REH‿ee [DAYL-lay BOO-stay].

591. —— some writing paper.
della carta da scrivere.
DAYL-lah KAHR-tah dah SKREE-vay-ray.

592. —— a fountain pen.
una penna stilografica.
OO-nah PAYN-nah stee-lo-GRAH-fee-kah.

593. —— a pencil.
una matita.
OO-nah mah-TEE-tah.

594. —— some picture postcards.
delle cartoline illustrate.
DAYL-lay kahr-toh-LEE-nay eel-loo-STRAH- tay.

595. —— some wrapping paper.
della carta da imballaggio.
DAYL-lah KAHR-tah dah eem-bahl-LAHJ-jo.

596. —— some string.
dello spago.
DAYL-lo SPAH-go.

CIGAR STORE

597. Where is the nearest cigar store?
Dov'è la tabaccheria più vicina?
doh-VEH lah tah-bahk-kay-REE-ah pyoo vee-CHEE- nah?

598. I want [some cigars].
Vorrei [dei sigari].
vohr-REH‿ee [day SEE-gah-ree].

599. —— a pack of American cigarettes.
un pacchetto di sigarette americane.
oon pahk-KAYT-toh dee see-gah-RAYT-tay ah- may-ree-KAH-nay.

600. —— a leather cigarette case.
un portasigarette di cuoio.
oon pohr-tah-see-gah-RAYT-tay dee KWAW- yoh.

601. —— a lighter.
un accendisigari.
oon ahch-chayn-dee-SEE-gah-ree.

602. —— some pipe tobacco.
del tabacco da pipa.
dayl tah-BAHK-ko dah PEE-pah.

603. Do you have a match?
Avrebbe un fiammifero?
ah-VREB-bay oon fyahm-MEE-fay-ro?

CAMERA SHOP

604. I want a roll of movie film for this camera.
Vorrei un rullo di pellicole cinematografiche per questa macchina.
vohr-REH‿ee oon ROOL-lo dee pel-LEE-ko-lay chee- nay-mah-toh-GRAH-fee-kay payr KWAY-stah MAHK-kee-nah.

605. What is the charge for developing a roll of color film?
Quanto costa la sviluppo di un rullo di fotografie a colori?
KWAHN-toh KAW-stah lo zvee-LOOP-po dee oon ROOL-lo dee fo-toh-grah-FEE-ay ah ko-LO-ree?

606. When will it be ready?
Quando sarà pronto?
KWAHN-doh sah-RAH PROHN-toh?

607. May I take a snapshot of you?
Posso farle un'istantanea?
PAWS-so FAHR-lay oo-nee-stahn-TAH-nay-ah?

DRUGSTORE

608. Where is a drugstore where they understand English?
Dov'è una farmacia dove capiscono l'inglese?
doh-VEH OO-nah fahr-mah-CHEE-ah doh-vay kah- PEE-sko-no leen-GLAY-zay?

609. May I speak to [a male clerk] a female clerk?
Potrei parlare con [un commesso] una commessa?
po-TREH‿ee pahr-LAH-ray kohn [oon kohm-MAYS- so] OO-nah kohm-MAYS-sah?

610. Can you fill this prescription immediately?
Mi può preparare questa ricetta subito?
mee pwaw pray-pah-RAH-ray KWAY-stah ree-CHET- tah SOO-bee-toh?

611. Do you have [some adhesive tape]?
Ha [del nastro adesivo]?
ah [dayl NAH-stro ah-day-ZEE-vo]?

612. —— some antiseptic. del disinfettante.
dayl dee-zeen-fayt-TAHN-tay.

613. —— some aspirin. dell'aspirina.
dayl-lah-spee-REE-nah.

614. —— a hairbrush. un spazzola pei capelli.
OO-nah SPAHT-tso-lah pay kah-PAYL-lee.

615. —— **a toothbrush.** uno spazzolino da denti.
OO-no spaht-tso-LEE-no dah DEN-tee.

616. —— **a comb.** un pettine. *oon PET-tee-nay.*

617. —— **a deodorant.** del deodorante.
dayl day-o-doh-RAHN-tay.

618. —— **a mild laxative.** un lassativo.
oon lahs-sah-TEE-vo.

619. —— **a razor.** un rasoio. *oon rah-ZO-yoh.*

620. —— **some razor blades.** delle lamette.
DAYL-lay lah-MET-tay.

621. —— **some sanitary napkins.**
dei pannolini igienici.
day pahn-no-LEE-nee ee-JYEH-nee-chee.

622. —— **a sedative.** un calmante.
oon kahl-MAHN-tay.

623. —— **some shampoo.** dello shampoo.
DAYL-lo "shampoo."

624. —— **some shaving cream (brushless).**
della crema da barba (senza pennello).
DAYL-lah KREH-mah dah BAHR-bah (SEN-tsah payn-NEL-lo).

625. —— **a thermometer.** un termometro.
oon tayr-MAW-may-tro.

626. —— **a tube of toothpaste.**
un tubetto di pasta dentifricia.
oon too-BAYT-toh dee PAH-stah dayn-tee-FREE-chyah.

LAUNDRY AND DRY CLEANING

627. Where is [the laundry]?
Dov'è [la lavanderia]?
doh-VEH [lah lah-vahn-day-REE-ah]?

628. —— the dry cleaner. la lavatura a secco.
lah lah-vah-TOO-rah ah SAYK-ko.

629. I want these shirts [washed].
Vorrei far [lavare] queste camicie.
vohr-REH‿ee fahr [lah-VAH-ray] KWAY-stay kah- MEE-chay.

630. —— mended.
rammendare.
rahm-mayn-DAH-ray.

631. No starch.
Niente amido.
NYEN-tay AH-mee-doh.

632. I want them starched.
Le vorrei inamidate.
lay vohr-REH‿ee ee-nah-mee-DAH-tay.

633. I want this suit [cleaned].
Vorrei far [pulire a secco] quest'abito.
vohr-REH‿ee fahr [poo-LEE-ray ah SAYK-ko] kway- STAH-bee-toh.

634. —— pressed.
stirare.
stee-RAH-ray.

635. The belt is missing.
La cintura manca.
lah cheen-TOO-rah MAHN-kah.

636. Can you sew on this button?
Mi può attaccare questo bottone?
mee pwaw aht-tahk-KAH-ray KWAY-stoh boht-TOH- nay?

637. Can you replace a zipper?
Può cambiarmi questa chiusura lampo?
pwaw kahm-BYAHR-mee KWAY-stah kyoo-ZOO-rah LAHM-po?

BARBERSHOP AND BEAUTY PARLOR

638. Where is [a beauty parlor]?
Dov'è [un parrucchiere]?
doh-VEH [oon pahr-rook-KYEH-ray]?

639. —— a barbershop.
un barbiere.
oon bahr-BYEH-ray.

640. A haircut, please.
Mi tagli i capelli, per favore.
mee TAH-lyee ee kah-PAYL-lee, payr fah-VO-ray.

641. Do not cut it too short.
Non li tagli troppo corti.
nawn lee TAH-lyee TRAWP-po KOHR-tee.

642. No lotion, please.
Niente lozione, per favore.
NYEN-tay lo-TSYOH-nay, payr fah-VO-ray.

643. A shave.
Mi faccia la barba.
mee FAHCH-chyah lah BAHR-bah.

644. A shampoo.
Mi lavi i capelli.
mee LAH-vee ee kah-PAYL-lee.

645. A hair set.
Mi metta in piega i capelli.
mee MET-tah in PYEH-gah ee kah-PAYL-lee.

646. A permanent.
Mi faccia una permanente.
mee FAHCH-chyah oo-nah payr-mah-NEN-tay.

647. A manicure.
Mi faccia le unghie.
mee FAHCH-chyah lay OON-gyay.

648. A massage.
Mi faccia un massaggio.
mee FAHCH-chyah oon mahs-SAHJ-jo.

649. A facial.
Mi faccia un massaggio alla faccia.
mee FAHCH-chyah oon mahs-SAHJ-jo AHL-lah FAHCH-chyah.

HEALTH AND ILLNESS

650. I wish to see an American doctor.
Vorrei avere un medico americano.
vohr-REH‿ee ah-VAY-ray oon MEH-dee-ko ah-may- ree-KAH-no.

651. Is the doctor in?
C'è il dottore?
cheh eel doht-TOH-ray?

652. I have [a headache].
Ho [un mal di testa].
aw [oon mahl dee TAY-stah].

653. —— an allergy. un'allergia.
oo-nahl-layr-JEE-ah.

654. —— a cold. un raffreddore.
oon rahf-frayd-DOH-ray.

655. —— a cough. la tosse. *lah TOHS-say.*

656. —— constipation. un imbarazzo di stomaco.
oon eem-bah-RAHT-tso dee STAW-mah-ko.

657. —— diarrhea. la diarrea. *lah dyahr-REH-ah.*

658. —— indigestion. un'indigestione.
oo-neen-dee-jay-STYOH-nay.

659. —— fever. la febbre. *lah FEB-bray.*

660. —— nausea. la nausea. *lah NAH‿oo-zay-ah.*

661. —— a sore throat. un mal di gola.
oon mahl dee GO-lah.

662. There is something in my eye.
Ho qualche cosa nell'occhio.
aw KWAHL-kay KAW-zah nayl-LAWK-kyoh.

663. I have a pain in my chest.
Ho un dolore al petto.
aw oon doh-LO-ray ahl PET-toh.

664. I did not sleep well.
Non ho dormito bene.
nawn aw dohr-MEE-toh BEH-nay.

665. I feel [better] worse.
Mi sento [meglio] peggio.
mee SEN-toh [MEH-lyoh] PEJ-jo.

666. Must I stay in bed?
Devo stare a letto?
DAY-vo STAH-ray ah LET-toh?

667. When will I be able to travel again?
Quando sarò in condizione di riprendere il viaggio?
KWAHN-doh sah-RAW een kohn-dee-TSYOH-nay dee ree-PREN-day-ray eel VYAHJ-jo?

DENTIST

668. Do you know a good dentist?
Conosce un buon dentista?
ko-NO-shay oon bwawn dayn-TEE-stah?

669. This tooth hurts.
Questo dente mi duole.
KWAY-stoh DEN-tay mee DWAW-lay.

670. Can you fix it temporarily?
Lo può accomodare provvisoriamente?
lo pwaw ahk-ko-mo-DAH-ray prohv-vee-zo-ryah- MAYN-tay?

671. I seem to have lost a filling.
Mi sembra che sia caduta l'impiombatura.
mee saym-brah kay SEE-ah kah-DOO-tah leem-pyohm- bah-TOO-rah.

672. I do not want the tooth extracted.
Non voglio che mi estragga il dente.
nawn VAW-lyoh kay mee ay-STRAHG-gah eel DEN- tay.

CONVERSATION AT THE POST OFFICE

673. Per favore, mi potrebbe dire quanti francobolli ci vogliono per mandare questa lettera negli Stati Uniti?
Could you please tell me how many stamps I need to send this letter to the United States?

674. Un francobollo da sessanta (60) lire se va per posta semplice. Per via aerea, invece, costa cento venti lire (120) ogni cinque grammi.
One stamp for 60 lire, if it goes by regular mail. By airmail, instead, it costs 120 lire for every five grams.

675. Allora, mi dia dieci (10) francobolli da sessanta (60) e cinque (5) da cento venti (120).
Well then, give me ten 60 lire stamps and five at 120.

676. Ecco qua. Dieci (10) da sessanta (60), cinque (5) da cento (100), e cinque (5) da venti (20); non ci sono francobolli da cento venti lire. Fa mille duecento (1,200) in tutto.
Here you are. Ten at 60 lire, five at a 100, and five at 20; there are no 120 lire stamps. That is 1,200 in all.

677. Grazie. E un'altra cosa, per favore. Dove posso fare la spedizione di questo pacco?
Thank you. And another thing, please. Where can I mail this package?

678. Lo dia a me. Ci penso io. Che cosa contiene? Niente di fragile?
Give it to me. I'll take care of it. What does it contain? Anything fragile?

679. Contiene solo libri. It contains only books.

680. Libri nuovi? New books?

681. No. Però vorrei assicurare il pacco. Quant'è la tariffa?
No. But I should like to insure the package. What is the rate?

682. Cinquanta (50) lire per un valore di dieci mila (10,000) lire.
Fifty lire per 10,000 value.

683. Vorrei assicurarlo per quaranta mila (40,000) lire.
I want to insure it for 40,000 lire.

684. Vuole riempire questo modulo? Fa quattrocento cinquanta (450) lire in tutto. Duecento cinquanta (250) per i francobolli e due cento (200) di sopratassa per l'assicurazione.
Will you fill in this form? It is 450 lire altogether. 250 for postage and an extra charge of 200 for the insurance.

685. Mi può dare una ricevuta?
May I have a receipt?

686. Certo. Per favore, la sua firma qui. C'è una buca per le lettere laggiù, a destra.
Of course. Please (put) your signature here. There's a letter box down there, on the right.

687. Grazie tanto.
Thanks very much.

CONVERSATION AT THE TELEPHONE

688. Per favore mi dia l'interurbana.
Please give me Long Distance.

689. Interurbana.
Long Distance.

690. Per favore mi dia Roma, otto cinque sei sette nove (85679).
Please give me Rome, 85679.

691. Il suo numero?
Your number?

692. Milano cinque quattro tre sette otto (54378). Quanto costa per i primi tre minuti?
Milano 54378. What is the charge for the first three minutes?

693. Quattrocento trenta (430) lire. Aspetti un momento che le dò la comunicazione. Eccola.
Four hundred thirty lire. Wait a moment for the connection. Here you are.

694. Pronto. Sono Giovanni Bianco; posso parlare con la signora Longhi?
Hello. This is Giovanni Bianco. May I speak to Mrs. Longhi?

695. Mi dispiace, non la capisco bene. Ci devono essere dei disturbi. Vuol parlare più forte?
I'm sorry. I don't understand you well. There must be some disturbance. Will you speak a little louder?

696. Sono Giovanni Bianco e desidero parlare con la signora Longhi.
This is Giovanni Bianco. I'd like to speak to Mrs. Longhi.

697. Mi dispiace, ma la signora Longhi non c'è. Dovrebbe essere di ritorno verso le nove.
I am sorry, Mrs. Longhi isn't in. She should be back by 9:00.

698. Vuol riferirle che ha chiamato Giovanni Bianco e che sarò in città domenica. La signora potrà chiamarmi domenica prima delle dieci all'Albergo Colonna. Il numero del telefono è cinque sei sette nove nove (56799), stanza sei cento due (602), sei cento due (602).
Will you tell her that Giovanni Bianco called and that I'll be in town Sunday. She can call me Sunday before 10:00 at Hotel Colonna. The telephone number is 56799, Room 602, 602.

699. Vada adagio che scrivo. Albergo Colonna, cinque sei sette nove nove (56799). Ha detto stanza cinque cento due (502)?
Speak slowly while I write. Hotel Colonna, 56799. Did you say Room 502?

700. No, stanza sei cento due (602), sei zero due (602).
No, Room 602, six-zero-two.

701. Va bene, ho capito.
All right, I understood.

702. Mi dispiace di averla incomodata. Grazie tanto.
I'm sorry to have bothered you. Thank you very much.

703. Oh, niente. Farò la sua ambasciata alla signora Longhi.
Oh, not at all. I'll give your message to Mrs. Longhi.

704. Grazie. Buon giorno.
Thanks. Goodbye.

705. Buon giorno.
Goodbye.

SENDING A CABLEGRAM

706. Desidererei inviare questo telegramma a New York.

Quanto costa?
I'd like to send this cablegram to New York City. How much does it cost?

707. **Il telegramma costa trenta (30) lire a parola.**
A cablegram costs 30 lire per word.

708. **C'è la solita tariffa minima per dieci parole?**
Is there the usual minimum charge for ten words?

709. **No, non c'è nessuna tariffa minima.**
No, there is no minimum charge.

710. **Si possono fare dei telegramma-lettera?**
Is it possible to send a lettergram?

711. **Sì. Costano metà tariffa con un minimo di ventidue (22) parole.**
Yes, they cost one-half rate with a minimum of 22 words.

712. **Quanto tempo impiega ad arrivare il telegramma-lettera?**
How long will it take for the lettergram to arrive?

713. **Non arriverebbe prima di domani pomeriggio.**
It would not arrive before tomorrow afternoon.

714. **E il telegramma quando arriverebbe?**
When would the cablegram arrive?

715. **In cinque ore circa.**
In about five hours.

716. **Allora decido per il telegramma. Mi dia dei moduli, per favore.**
Then I'll send a telegram. Give me some forms, please.

717. **Eccoli. Scriva il suo nome e l'indirizzo in stampatello, per piacere. Poi riporti il modulo a me, e ci penserò io.**
Here they are. Print your name and address please. Return the form to me and I'll take care of them.

718. **Grazie tanto.**
Thanks very much.

TIME

719. What time is it?
Che ora è?
kay O-rah eh?

720. It is (very) early.
È (molto) presto.
eh (MOHL-toh) PREH-stoh.

721. It is (quite) late.
È (abbastanza) tardi.
eh (ahb-bah-STAHN-tsah) TAHR-dee.

722. It is almost two o'clock (A.M.).
Sono quasi le due.
SO-no KWAH-zee lay DOO-ay.

723. It is two o'clock (P.M.).
Sono le quattordici.
SO-no lay kwaht-TAWR-dee-chee.

724. It is half-past three (P.M.).
Sono le quindici e mezzo.
SO-no lay KWEEN-dee-chee ay MED-dzo.

725. It is quarter-past four (P.M.).
Sono le sedici e un quarto.
SO-no lay SAY-dee-chee ay oon KWAHR-toh.

726. It is a quarter to five (P.M.).
Sono le diciassette meno un quarto.
SO-no lay dee-chyahs-SET-tay MAY-no oon KWAHR- toh.

727. It is ten minutes to six (P.M.).
Sono le diciotto meno dieci.
SO-no lay dee-CHYAW-toh MAY-no DYEH-chee.

728. At twenty minutes past seven (P.M.).
Alle diciannove e venti.
AHL-lay dee-chyahn-NAW-vay ay VAYN-tee.

729. In the morning.
Nella mattinata.
nayl-lah maht-tee-NAH-tah.

730. During the afternoon.
Nel pomeriggio.
nayl po-may-REEJ-jo.

731. In the evening.
In serata.
een say-RAH-tah.

732. Day. Giorno. *JOHR-no.*

733. Every night. Ogni notte. *O-nyee NAWT-tay.*

734. Last night.
Ieri sera.
YEH-ree SAY-rah.

735. Last month.
Il mese scorso.
eel MAY-zay SKOHR-so.

736. Last year.
L'anno scorso.
LAHN-no SKOHR-so.

737. Yesterday. Ieri. *YEH-ree.*

738. Today. Oggi. *AWJ-jee.*

739. Tonight. Stasera. *stah-SAY-rah.*

740. Tomorrow. Domani. *doh-MAH-nee.*

741. Next week.
La settimana prossima.
lah sayt-tee-MAH-nah PRAWS-see-mah.

DAYS OF THE WEEK

742. Monday. Lunedì. *loo-nay-DEE.*

743. Tuesday. Martedì. *mahr-tay-DEE.*

744. Wednesday. Mercoledì. *mayr-ko-lay-DEE.*

745. Thursday. Giovedì. *jo-vay-DEE.*

746. Friday. Venerdì. *vay-nayr-DEE.*

747. Saturday. Sabato. *SAH-bah-toh.*

748. Sunday. Domenica. *doh-MAY-nee-kah.*

MONTHS

749. January. Gennaio. *jayn-NAH-yoh.*

750. February. Febbraio. *fayb-BRAH-yoh.*

751. March. Marzo. *MAHR-tso.*

752. April. Aprile. *ah-PREE-lay.*

753. May. Maggio. *MAHJ-jo.*

754. June. Giugno. *JOO-nyoh.*

755. July. Luglio. *LOO-lyoh.*

756. August. Agosto. *ah-GO-sto.*

757. September. Settembre. *sayt-TEM-bray.*

758. October. Ottobre. *oht-TOH-bray.*

759. November. Novembre. *no-VEM-bray.*

760. December. Dicembre. *dee-CHEM-bray.*

SEASONS AND WEATHER

761. Spring. Primavera. *pree-mah-VEH-rah.*

762. Summer. Estate. *ay-STAH-tay.*

763. Autumn. Autunno. *ah‿oo-TOON-no.*

764. Winter. Inverno. *een-VEHR-no.*

765. It is warm. Fa caldo. *fah KAHL-doh.*

766. It is cold. Fa freddo. *fah FRAYD-doh.*

767. The weather is good. Fa bel tempo. *fah bel TEM-po.*

768. The weather is bad. Fa cattivo tempo. *fah kaht-TEE-vo TEM-po.*

769. It is still raining. Piove ancora. *PYAW-vay ahn-KO-rah.*

NUMBERS

770. Zero. Zero. *DZEH-ro.*

One. Uno. *OO-no.*

Two. Due. *DOO-ay.*

Three. Tre. *tray.*

Four. Quattro. *KWAHT-tro.*

Five. Cinque. *CHEEN-kway.*

Six. Sei. *SEH‿ee.*

Seven. Sette. *SET-tay.*

Eight. Otto. *AWT-toh.*

Nine. Nove. *NAW-vay.*

Ten. Dieci. *DYEH-chee.*

Eleven. Undici. *OON-dee-chee.*

Twelve. Dodici. *DOH-dee-chee.*

Thirteen. Tredici. *TRAY-dee-chee.*

Fourteen. Quattordici. *kwaht-TOHR-dee-chee.*

Fifteen. Quindici. *KWEEN-dee-chee.*

Sixteen. Sedici. *SAY-dee-chee.*

Seventeen. Diciassette. *dee-chyahs-SET-tay.*

Eighteen. Diciotto. *dee-CHYAWT-toh.*

Nineteen. Diciannove. *dee-chyahn-NAW-vay.*

Twenty. Venti. *VAYN-tee.*

Twenty-one. Ventuno. *vayn-TOO-no.*

Twenty-two. Ventidue. *vayn-tee-DOO-ay.*

Thirty. Trenta. *TRAYN-tah.*

Forty. Quaranta. *kwah-RAHN-tah.*

Fifty. Cinquanta. *cheen-KWAHN-tah.*

Sixty. Sessanta. *says-SAHN-tah.*

Seventy. Settanta. *sayt-TAHN-tah.*

Eighty. Ottanta. *oht-TAHN-tah.* **Ninety.** Novanta. *no-VAHN-tah.*

One hundred. Cento. *CHEN-toh.*

One hundred and one. Cento uno. *CHEN-toh OO-no.*

Two hundred. Duecento. *doo-ay-CHEN-toh.*

One thousand. Mille. *MEEL-lay.*

Two thousand. Due mila. *DOO-ay MEE-lah.*

One million. Un milione. *oon mee-LYOH-nay.*

INDEX

The sentences, words and phrases in this book are numbered consecutively from 1 to 770. All entries in this book refer to these numbers. In addition, each major section heading (CAPITALIZED) is indexed according to page number (**boldface**). Parts of speech are indicated by the following italic abbreviations: *adj.* for adjective, *adv.* for adverb, *n.* for noun and *v.* for verb. Parentheses are used for explanations.

Because of the large volume of material indexed, cross-indexing has generally been avoided. Phrases or groups of words will usually be found under only one of their components, e.g., "bathing suit" appears only under "bathing," even though there is a separate entry for "suit" alone. If you do not find a phrase under one word, try another.